Mrs. GreenJeans

Works out the Worries

(Coloring Book)

Mrs. GreenJeans

Works out the Worries

(Coloring Book)

Ebony Jackson Brown MSW, LCSW

Copyright

Printed in the United States of America

First Printing, 2017

ISBN-13: 978-0-9909919-1-5
ISBN10: 0990991911

References

Diagnostic and statistical manual of mental disorders fifth edition DSM-5 American psychiatric association

Greenberger, P. D., & Padesky, P. C. (1995). Mind Over Mood: Change How You Feel by Changing the Way You Think. New York: The Guilford Press.

The Butterfly Typeface Publishing
PO BOX 56193
Little Rock Arkansas 72215

Disclaimer

The *Mrs. GreenJeans* series is designed to provide information about the subject matter covered. It is sold with the understanding that the publisher and author are not engaged in rendering therapeutic professional services. If therapeutic assistance is required, the services of a competent and qualified professional should be sought.

Every effort has been made to make these books as complete and as accurate as possible. However, the information provided should not be considered as all inclusive. Therefore, this text should be used only as a general guide and not as the ultimate source of therapeutic information. Furthermore, these books contain information on therapeutic information and techniques only up to the printing date.

The purpose of these book is to educate and to entertain. The author and Butterfly Typeface Publishing shall have neither liability nor responsibility to any person or entity with respect to any loss or damage caused or alleged to be caused directly or indirectly by the information contained in these books.

For all those that struggle with anxiety.

"Deep Breathing, Challenging Your Thoughts."

-Mrs. GreenJeans

To my loving and supportive husband,
as well as our four children.

Look for other books in the

Mrs. GreenJeans

Series

Vocabulary

Sufficient   ⟶   Enough, adequate

Conquer   ⟶   Overcome

Probability ⟶ Likelihood something will happen

Detracts ⟶ Reduce value

Insecurities ⟶ Lack of confidence

"A person that searches for flaws in other people is only afraid that theirs will be discovered."

—Mrs. GreenJeans

"Stop assuming the worst about yourself, believe you are sufficient for those people meant to be in your life."

−Mrs. GreenJeans

"For as long as you live, you'll have flaws, that's because no one is perfect. Become comfortable with imperfection for it is what makes each of us uniquely beautiful."

-Mrs. GreenJeans

"The message
is always more
important than the
messenger.
Focus on the value of the
message,
then lose yourself in the
message to conquer your
anxiety."

−Mrs. GreenJeans

"What you think about
yourself is far more
important than what
anyone else thinks."

−Mrs. GreenJeans

"Personal opinions belong to the owner of the opinion."

-Mrs. GreenJeans

"A difficult day can create an easier tomorrow when you have learned what made the day difficult, and how to overcome it."

— Mrs. GreenJeans

"Losing sleep over a probability is a waste of a good night's rest especially the next day when you are too tired to maintain the worry."

—Mrs. GreenJeans

"Worry requires great imagination."

-Mrs. GreenJeans

"Worrying about what happened yesterday detracts from your opportunity to be great today."

—Mrs. Greenjeans

"Worry tries to make you afraid to own the moment, don't let worry cause you to miss an opportunity to inspire others."

— Mrs. GreenJeans

#ICOM

In Control of Me

"Bullies are people with insecurities that try to make other people feel insecure."

−Mrs. GreenJeans

The End

About the Author

Author Ebony Jackson Brown is a retired Air Force wife who began her career as a childcare provider for military families during her husband's career in 1995.

She later decided she wanted to care for military personnel and families in a different capacity and sought an education in social work. Ebony graduated with a bachelor's degree from Methodist University in the field of social work. Subsequently Ebony graduated from the University of Southern California earning a Master of Social Work Degree, with a concentration in mental health and military social work.

The series, *Mrs. GreenJeans,* highlights diversity as mental illness is not discriminatory among races, ethnicities, or culture. The books are a representation of the capacity to which therapists affect change and growth in individuals and highlights the importance of therapy in our society. Therapists are professionals whom individuals should seek for direction and support while attempting to navigate life's problematic circumstances and situations.

The goal of the *Mrs. GreenJeans* series (storybooks, workbooks, and activity books) is to combat the stigma of mental health services so that seeking and engaging in mental health services is normalized.

Ebony Jackson Brown continues to provide care to military personnel and their families as a licensed clinical social worker. She and her husband of 26 years reside in North Carolina with their four children.

Tops of The Trees Books

An imprint of Butterfly Typeface Publishing

WWW.BUTTERFLYTYPEFACE.COM

Made in the USA
Middletown, DE
24 February 2023

25549470R00027